Recapturing the Renaissance

Recapturing the Renaissance

YOLANDRA WOODS

ISBN: 978-1-64826-989-9   (Paperback Edition)
ISBN: 978-1-64826-990-5   (Hardcover Edition)
ISBN: 978-1-64826-988-2   (E-book Edition)

Some characters and events in this book are fictitious. Any similarity to real persons, living or dead, is coincidental and not intended by the author.

Book Ordering Information

Phone Number: 347-901-4929 or 347-901-4920
Email: info@globalsummithouse.com
Global Summit House
www.globalsummithouse.com

Printed in the United States of America

Contents

Recapturing the Renaissance is an inspirational poetry book that was written to inspire people of all ages. This book consists of seventy-eight pages.

This book deals with poetry on an internal and external reality of life situations and feelings. It was written based on many stories that were shared looking for answers or an ear to listen and express feelings.

The goal is to reach the hearts of many who are broken, to free their minds and hearts because many may be dealing with the same issues but have never been released to be delivered and set free.

Acknowledgments

I have been blessed to have known many people who have influenced my life, and I am overwhelmed that God has placed them in my life to stand by me.

To my siblings, Kim, Sabrina, Roshawn, and Dasia, and my brother, Divine, I thank you all for listening to me, my ideas and stories, even when you were tired.

Thank you for never giving up on me but inspiring me. I want you all to know we are fortunate to be raised by our parents. Our unity made family closeness the first factor in our lives, for a family that prays together stays together.

I thank all who will read this book and be inspired by the emotions, feelings, and situations that will make you wiser and heal some wounds and think about the choices you made.

I could not be more grateful than to have two extended brothers: Gino Hudson, who stepped in when my dad died as a support and mentor to all when times were rough. I couldn't ask for a better brother to love my sister and take on her family when times were hard too. As you would say, you didn't know you had so many wives. LOL.

Benny Timmons Jr., who was there throughout my teenage years encouraging me to be strong and was a true uncle to my kids. I thank you for you have a heart of gold.

To my mom, Mary Woods, I love you because you carried me in your womb. You are my number one favorite girl and couldn't ask for a better mother. I'm so grateful God created you just for me.

Thank you, God.

Special thanks to Pastor Joseph Cook and the beautiful woman who stands behind him, First Lady Hattie Cook, for preaching faith without works is dead; Min. Katherine Timmons who has been my spiritual mother and who has deposited so much word and encouragement into my life; Alberta Timmons for her listening ears through the late nights; and Carolyn Alston for she holds a special place in my heart from childhood to adulthood. I thank you for being in my life. I greatly appreciate every one of you.

I, Yolandra Woods Timmons, was born and raised in Brooklyn, New York, and now reside in Norlina, North Carolina. I attended Fashion Industries High School / Thomas Jefferson where I finished and then took on a career as a cosmetologist.

I am a woman of my word, with a love and passion to help others. I am a devoted mother of three beautiful children: Wayne Timmons Jr., Tywayne Timmons, and Skylia Timmons. Wayne and Tywayne, I love you like only a mom would. You are two young men with the same mom and dad but are different in so many ways, that's why it's important that I must empower you to understand that you are different children but have unique ways that only a mom could understand. There is enough love that I have instilled in you to grow and extend the love to others, for I pray. I can't teach you to be a man, but you shall know how to treat your wife and how you want to be treated. Skylia Timmons, my daughter, you are a gift from God, unique from the womb, just blessed as you were delivered with a cardiac problem of an overrated heartbeat. I now understand why you were put to the test. Your talents and gifts had been already blessed, and I am enjoying watching you as you grow, my little diamond.

Wayne Timmons Sr., my husband, who blessed me with three beautiful bundles of joy, we have endured so much together, for our love has been put to the test. Thank you for loving me.

Publishers, I thank you.
Tywayne Timmons/Book Cover/design
Author Yolandra Woods

CHAPTER 1

External and Internal Reality of Life Situations

A Father's Love

It was my dad who died yesterday. I take his knowledge and wisdom and share, to sit back and realize the things he could no longer bear.

The love of his family he knew cares, the hurt of knowing one day he wouldn't be there.

It's so hard to explain the tears no one sees, his pride is what hurt, and no one could imagine how hard it must be.

I remember those days all he did is be supportive in all, we done raised five girls and had one son.

Humble man in Christ, it was God who knew it was time to shorten his life.

A love of a father.

A Mother's Love

I love him he is my child
I love him he is my only boy
I love him I don't want to live
With the pain to face the reality
I don't know how to help
I feel so ashamed
I love him how can I let him
Go, he's a grown man, but I'm hurting
So
I love him I can't be at peace
Can't let him be lost to the streets
I love him it's been nine months of
stretching my womb to fear
Your life flash before your eyes
Thirty years later is too soon.
She loves him but no one knows
the price to love a child so dear
to put yourself in harm just to
Keep him near.

Yolandra Woods

Sisters

Love thy sisters.
For they may haven't had a choice.
God has chosen the family to be in
your life, for we were born into this
family who knows if it was right?
     I had no choice to love them
but I am so pleased, he blessed me
with a loving family
who could believe.
It's like the flowers
that bloom in the morning glow
as the sunshine I want the world.
to know how beautiful and grateful
I am to have all of you as apart
of me I'd travel the world to show
how much you mean to me and
express the importance of family.

Family

What about the good old days
Mama in the kitchen cooking rice,
preparing meals for the family that
was right, Papa at work making
the bread, children in school filling
their heads, counting down the hours
to come home and spread the
love of a family and be fed a
good meal at the table before
they say their daily bread.

Friends

A friend is one who will be
around.
A friend is one who never lets
you down
A friend will build you up when
you're weak
A friend is one who got your
back when you fall.
A friend will be there during hard
times when you call.
A friend will go through the extreme
to keep the relationship tight, and
handle situations when trials may
come your way. Friendship is
genuine and it's just no more
to say real friends don't come easy so if you
have one I pray that it continues to grow.

Marriage

When I hear the word *marriage*
I hear a team under a holy communion
of two joined together as one, woman and man
building a foundation to share the dream of two
in love that cared enough to combine their lives as one
and share honesty and trust with a commitment for better
or for worst so that when trials come their way the unity
would be so tight they would be able to bare for one day one
may leave in death but know it was love that carried them
through, but death took them apart for they held on to marriage
vows that were true love, patience, trust, and honesty we must practice
for marriage to stay true.

Yolandra Woods

Love Me While I'm Here

Love me while I'm here
for when I'm gone it will be nothing
you could do.
        Love me while I'm here and cry
tears of happiness and pain.
        Love me while I'm here
for you have time now
but tomorrow is numbered
love me while I'm here for time
is available to you, to show how
much you care.
        Love me while I'm here so there will
be thoughts or wishes you could have
shared. Love me now for your
memories will cause you no pain
and be free of your conscience
to let go but in your heart I'd know
you love me so.

The Heat

I was the candle he was
the fire, it was love on fire
always turned on as the candle
Lit with blazing flames
Love on fire makes you want to stay
out the streets, no heartaches.
No pains, constant heat, running to
get home don't want to be alone
thinking he called, the sweet
smell as the candle gradually fades away.
Love on fire want it to
last forever, too hot to handle dancing,
romancing, hugging each other,
loving each other, it was love on fire,
blazing with flame.

Yolandra Woods

The Day

The first day I felt the
gift that God had given me
which was the gift to produce
children. It filled my life with
joy and the grateful thing of all
was he blessed me with two
beautiful boys and a girl.
The day
I saw you smile.
You gave me so much hope.
The day you walked
it encouraged me to strive harder
The day you talked
it gave me the wisdom
to speak words of knowledge so you
would grow from an infant to a child.
From a young man to one day a man.
From that day you changed my
life and I will continue to love you
and give you a good life.

CHAPTER 2

Soul Cleansing—
Releasing the Cause of the Problem

What If

Imagine if you were a fish.
If I were a fish
I would swim as if every day
I would have a chance to be
purified and new
And if I were a bird
I would fly so high in the
sky to be free
And if I were a tree as the
seasons change I'd be shedding
leaves for newness as the wind
blows. Shifting in the air.
I'd be swimming becoming
a new, flying to be free
blowing in the air
And if I were the world
you could not identify me.

As I Lay Down to Sleep

As I lay my head down to sleep
my heart continues to beat,
as time goes by, afraid of the dreams that
maybe. Something that causes me fear,
seeing things I don't want to see.
Afraid to go to sleep so I began
to keep my Bible near praying to God
for another peaceful sleep that
won't allow my dreams to cause
me any fears. And wake up in
a sweat filled with tears.

Hiding behind the Shadow

Criticizing and analyzing
others, blessings
living life in my shadow's
directions.
Walking earth like I'm cursed
seeking higher power
when pain hurts
I lurk and portray
to play these games.
Changing my face
but only the pigment
of my skin remains
the same.

Lies

He lies, she lies, why lie,
one lie will lead to a
second lie, the second lie
will lead to the third,
and at that point there's no need
to try for the truth, don't stand a chance
when you constantly lie
A lie can cause you to hurt
the one you love.
A lie can cause trouble that you
can never imagine and life just won't
be the same.
A lie can cause the fears of your
life to turn into a life full of
guilt and shame and by the time
you realize you need to tell
the truth no one believes you and
who do you blame?

Yolandra Woods

Blame Game

Everyone is looking for someone
to blame. From the young girl having a
baby with the shame.
To the young man who chose the
gang 'cause he says he has no family,
yet everyone wants to blame.
The father who's fatherless, who sees himself
as no good, the mother who's motherless
feels she doesn't have a chance 'cause she
grew up in the hood, everyone looking for
the chance, to place the blame for their
thoughts are like tragedy, negative confusing,
it's like an explosion that's waiting to happen,
the blame game, he did it, she did it,
but what did you do, everyone is
looking for someone to blame.

Sympathy

As I look upon thy face
the feeling of love was not a trace
in need of a healing
Like no one knows
the anger upon thy face
it really shows
The fear of who you are
the pain of whom they want
to be, it's the failures that
everyone sees.
No one to relate with
what I feel, no love,
no glory, this is a sinner's
story.

The Whisper

They whisper
I am a child
They whisper,
I want things to fade away as adults
talk about parents to children in a bad
way.
They whisper as my heart skips a
beat.
There is nothing I could say, they whisper
about my parents, it hurts so deep
They whisper I must respect my
Elders, I can't speak.
I don't want to hear, all I could do
is shed tears as they whisper about
my parents, it's a war being trapped between
obstacles
I fear, they are trying to destroy what's so
dear, these are my parents and I can't
speak how must I go on with so much
animosity this is family
I thought they cared I am a child, it's too much for me.

Break the Chain

Could you imagine
what it's like to be a single mom?
Raising the children alone
wondering if she could make it,
unable to break the chain of life
through family curses of being that
single mom caught up from man
to man, looking for love in all
the wrong places had to bare a
child with many faces battling
the struggle to climb through
the challenges of life and break
through the chains that cursed
your life. Breaking the chain
by educating, motivating your children
teaching self-worth so they could
be free and not end up with
many babies man after man
but protect their body so when
they do get impregnated they'd know the
daddy.

Yolandra Woods

Young Man

Living with the struggles
of a black man.
Torn by the color of their skin,
no one wants to take the time
to realize the person that lives
within. Always had to create the
image to be tough just to keep
from getting punked, Daddy always
said to man up and quit acting
like a girl, never loving or hugging
it's a hard-core world, young
male classified as doing crimes
getting paid little as nothing, living
on a dime, child support payments
missed will have you doing time.
Young men, you got to keep
your head above water and pay
so you don't have to live behind
a cell, angry man will have
you in jail.

Violence

Thoughts in my head
as tears begin to shed.
Every time you turn on the news
there's another one dead.
Pain in my heart.
Of constant hearing about shots
how can a world turn to such high
crime, all I could do is try to
protect mine.
Anger on the streets
my heart skips a beat with the fear
of violence but what happened to the
love that kept the peace.

Running

Shall I hide in the shadow
where no one knows
who I am or should I
run the chaotic streets, until
my mind goes blink
shall I hide in the darkness
behind the shame of all society
pressures you to be?
Running, running from the fears
trying to escape from your
past, from house to house
running in silence and no one
has a clue why you are there
the reality of it is when you
ever slow down, the hurt is
still there, the problem is still there
so stand through the test
and be strong to stop running
so it won't last long.

Tempted

Looking Good

Are you tempted?
tempted by the baggie jeans
nice clean-cut biceps triceps
handsomely dressed? Yes, it was
my flesh.
    Timberland boots wearing,
knew how to talk the talk
thought he had a head on his
shoulders. Oops! He lied, been
in the game long, he was just older.
    Thought he was mine,
news flash, he was just buying time.
    Didn't know it was sin that
let him in. I was tempted by
Satan that caught my eyes,
it was darkness that made me blind.

Yolandra Woods

Contaminated Love

It was love that contaminated
my ability to live.
Like bad food entering your body
through your bloodstream.
It was contaminated love
that caused me to be weak
blocked my mind with confusion
until I couldn't speak.
Contaminated love it was
that caused me to fall
struggling to give my all
it was contaminated love that
caused me to be bitter when I
knew it wasn't healthy for me
contaminated love used my mind
hurt my body, now I'm so broken.
Listen to these words as they're being spoken
so don't be a victim of contaminated love.

CHAPTER 3

Reflection of Inflection—Looking at the Situation

And It Was Love

It was love that entered
tragedies, disappointments,
and failures into my life.
Unable to connect my soul with
the true meaning of love.
Previous situations allow you to
build a wall, disconnect yourself
from that beautiful thing they call
love.
It was love that lied to me
It was love that hurt me
it was love that caused me pain
and last but not least love
just left me behind.
So tell me what about that
thing they call love.

The Vision

To see a vision of someone
who looks familiar to you.
I don't know could it be me.
So drained emotionally can't define
who it must be.
That vision in the mirror resembles me,
so lost in time.
Stole everything, your self-esteem,
ability to love, no, it's not fine.

The vision of a woman who can't
identify who she is or who she needs
to be, she has divorced herself
from her own body.
Emotionally wounded for so long
her mind was programmed to feel
it wasn't wrong.
Let go and please allow yourself
to move on.

Yolandra Woods

He Smiles / She Smiles

The smile was as beautiful
as a shade of gold,
But the story was never told.
Living the life of a struggle only
to hide behind a smile that
was as bright as gold, behind
closed doors they lived a life.
Of poverty, but because of her
dignity, pride, they smiled knowing
times were hard and could
barely provide.
As a voice was heard that
spoke the words *seek thee first*
it was the father saying you must
thirst. Unaware of what that must
mean, but he spoke clearly even
through a dream that allowed them
to see their purpose in life and
journey.

When Love Has No Meaning

When love has no meaning
things that used to hurt doesn't
seem to hurt anymore.
When love has no meaning you
spend less time weeping
When love has no meaning you
feel an emptiness to shed no
tears,
When love has no meaning you're
ready to face all fears.
When love has no meaning everything
seems to fade away.
When love has no meaning it just
doesn't matter you have nothing but silence.

Yolandra Woods

Shattered

My windows have been shaken
but now it's broken and shattered
with glass, every part of my mind,
body, and soul has been broken down.
Like the glass on my window ledge
so broken, I feel as if I'm gonna
go off the edge; but yet I recognize
windows can be replaced, and don't
remain broken, but be replaced as new.
The windows of my life I'm trying
to fix but there are some pieces that
are missing and there is no one who
wants to listen, but I'm shattered
like the broken glass, and even as
you try to walk in newness there
is always someone there to help
you remember the past.

CHAPTER 4

Break Free

Looking in the Eyes of Sin

When I look into your eyes
dodging the rays that glide
encouraging me to lie.
I see my sin in which I abide
but hide because my faith
Entitles me to be blind
Even though I've crossed the line
this fury drives a vibe sending an illusion
that I have sinned and must die
being a victim for sin lies in the
eyes for flesh has taken over my
faith, help me I cry, I cry
please, Lord, I don't want to die.

Battle of the Mind

In my mind it's a critical
weapon never neglecting, respecting
a lifetime of when I was an
adolescent.
Counting my blessings
feeling to choose my confession
relying on substance
no conscience.
Thinking recivily to a certain
extent looking back my head
was as hard as cement.
Never listening for Mom had
my back even when Dad attacked
hard to break my thoughts,
said we must make our own
mistakes. A life challenge of
lessons thank God I'm a blessing.

Suicidal Thoughts

You grab that knife and put it
to your veins

Hoping when you die you won't
feel the same only not to know
how you'd feel if you're gone,
You pop pills just to ease your
pain looking out the windows.
late nights as it rains.
Sitting back reminiscing on
mistakes that led you to this
state of mind
The actions you take to hurt
yourself is still committing a crime.
Time begins to pass by you begin
to cry asking yourself why? Why?
Someone's coming in, suck it up.
Holding it inside as you get older
your heart gets colder, my God I need
a shoulder, so you lean to the closest
person to you but it didn't work, drowning
in tears don't be a victim of murder you're
just killing fears.

They Thought They Cursed My Life

They thought they cursed my life with
words of discouragement that could
ruin my life.
They thought they cursed my life
who would have thought even family
don't always wish you well and say
things harmful that remain as a young
child growing up; they never encouraged
me with words of wisdom to grow
and be a man, not looking for sympathy
just looking for a helping hand.
They thought they cursed my life don't
want to be a victim of jail to repeat
the cycle of family members making
others' lives a living hell.
They thought they cursed my life because
of my disability to learn, it's my desire
to earn the right to be a perfect male.
They thought they cursed my life
but someone was praying day and night.

Yolandra Woods

How Many Times Will I Accept Your Apology?

You apologized once
and I accepted to let you know I care.
You apologize twice
I accepted hoping we would move on.
You apologize a third time,
I realize it was my low self-esteem
that kept accepting your apology but
now it's time I move on.
How many times must I accept
your apology when you know you're wrong?
How many times must I accept your apology
to keep me holding on accepting, thinking
it's a form of love but yet it was
a form of allowing you to do what you do?
I apologized to myself so now
Your apology is finished. I'm through.

Overwhelmed

Overwhelmed with myself with all the things I have
been through, hiding behind the mask of the truth
looking in the mirror of the room it's like you imprisoned
yourself to this sinful world being trapped with a heart
to do right but a mind to do wrong many may face
but the reality is you can't live in an unstable life to
win the race so I kill my thoughts of the negative
as I begin to scream let me out! Let me out! There
is no way I can allow my thoughts to make me burn i
n hell for my heart is good but recognizing my heart
and mind needs to be on one accord in order to be
at peace. Overwhelmed with myself for facing the reality
of the truth, I did it, and so could you

The World

       The world we live in can take
a life and amazing God than gives
one back.
       The world can kill your people
through violence, physical, financial,
verbal, and even now political
that's a fact.
       It's a credibility
to create something
which we as a people can only dream
people hate the world which they live in
feeling like to live in such a beautiful
world but live such a life of hate
causes our people to hate from the
pain that lives inside
As the world turns it's like it's watching
us as we sleep can't predict what
can take place for yet murder now
happens in your sleep, but yet it's me
against the world until I face defeat
for I weep the sorrow of our people
as we walk these streets.

Memory

Don't want to live the memory
of who I used to be.
What a life
I close my eyes to deposit
the energy from hurt to pain.
From tears to my fears,
My God what a memory.
I suffered a long life of not loving
me sacrificing for others,
who were too blind to see.
What a memory
I close my eyes to the death
of my past, thank God it didn't last.

Yolandra Woods

To Grieve

I have died inside
but I need to grieve that part of
me.
    To die inside because of all your
past memories of holding on so long
it's wrong to allow yourself to
suffer with the pain.
    To die inside is no one to blame.
but you, for this loss but it's a price
you pay and it's a heavy cost.
    I have died inside the reality
of trying to get back where you need
need to be but I give thanks
because now I'm free.

Too Strong

Living a life with many secrets.
Hiding emotions and feelings.
Still have no weakness.

Heart has been broken down with
hurt and pain but still stand strong
for I remain.

Torn apart broken but yet my heart
has been rebuilt to stand, strong

So yes, I have a purpose in life
and that's to live on.

So do I live or die? By becoming
empowered by my own integrity.

Yolandra Woods

One Life

One life to live.
So I try to live it to the fullest.
I must conquer an obstacle to
fulfill the dreams, but with the world
being toxic and filled with tragic
seems like it's gonna take magic
you get sucked in like water evaporated
by the sun, wondering what happened
to the dream.
The world is like leaking gases.
So I try to stay with the passion
to go hard and dodge the crashes
or remain still like traffic
to devour a life that was always
unlasting.

Tears

Tears on my pillow
Covered like rain heart
So heavy crying through the pain.
trying to stay strong
pressing and holding, the pillow
as tears are rolling down my
face saddened by so many issues
mine, yours, even the neighbor
next door but yet I thank
God for his grace that shall follow
all the days of our lives.
And as the tears fall on my pillow
I ask for mercy through the night.
        A pillow of tears poured down
like rain but yet grace and
mercy still remain.

Yolandra Woods

The Sunset

As the sun sets
I begin to rise
rise from the emotional
battles of life's challenges
as the sun sets
I think back to all the times
of no smiles, laughter, or joy
As the sun sets it's a beautiful
sight to see couldn't capture the
beauty because of being so unhappy
The world changes but a life of
a psycho that repeats itself time
after time we must not accept the
dark cloud but accept the sun as
it sets.

What Happened

       What happened to the hopscotch,
red rover, and red light green light
one, two, three games children played.
       What happened to the thirteen-inch
black-and-white TV we watched in the
living room as a family
       Technology took over with the
big screen to flat screen.
       What happened to that look that
the parents gave that the child knew.
They were almost as good as dead
what happened to the neighbor that
looked over the kids and didn't
care what was said.
       What happened to the teacher
that would fight for our children
without any fears.
       Why is it that now it seems
as if no one cares
       What happened.

       Yolandra Woods

Have You Noticed Our Children

What happened to our children?

Behavior problems got them medicated
with drugs.
Parents no longer able to discipline
have to practice tough love.
What happened to our children?
Criminal minds got them doing time.
Discipline was a factor to
keep our children out of jail
but society rates it as abuse, children
causing hell.
Teachers no longer able to control
the students, no one has respect.
Their passion for teaching has been
put to the test, teachers sleeping
with students, then you have
the issue of rape, some are
real and others are an escape.
What happened to our children
two parents were in the home
now children are left alone
for both parents have to work
to make incomes meet.
Children raising children now
they're hanging in the streets
left alone now your girl
child is pregnant but yet
no one could afford to stay
home

Young man in school, don't have
a dime now have to pay child
support or will be doing time.

What happened to our children
messed up, drugged up, knocked
up, or locked up.

What happened to our
children?

Yolandra Woods

Prayer Changes Things

I was a sinner
who prayed
that one day all the pain,
hurt, and sorrow would fade away
and my tomorrow would no longer
look like yesterday
I had no sword
but I knew how to pray
and with that prayer he
gave me power so now I
stand here looking forward to
tomorrow

Release the Tears

Have you ever cried because
of all the pain you felt inside
the thought of all the times
you embraced people whom you
thought can appreciate who you
are?
Unaware of the problems and trials
you had to face, it was Gods armor
and shield that allowed me to run
this race.
I cried the reality of trying to
convince yourself these things weren't
real the length of time holding on
to the way people really feel about you/me
is what killed the part of me to be me
so yesterday I cried.

Yolandra Woods

The Storm

Like a storm, we face
confusion, destruction, and things
unexplained
    We all have once experienced
Life's challenges of love, arguments
separations, and deaths
    The storm never once prepared
to have a time or place and at
times the storm can't be traced
    The storm seems as if it
will never end don't know the place
it started or when it will end.

CHAPTER 5

Rescued

It Was Jesus

It was Jesus who forgave me
of my sins
Jesus allowed me to love again.
Jesus never told my secret
Jesus is my personal keeper
Jesus fought my battles when
I couldn't fight.
Jesus, he's all right.
My Jesus.

When I Think

When I think of God
I think of Jesus
When I think of Jesus
I think of the Lord
When I think of the Lord
I think of the heavens
When I think of the heavens
I think of me, myself, and I
and when I think of me, myself,
and I, I think of you.

The First to Say Goodbye

No one wants to be the first
to say goodbye.
The first one is always considered,
to be the blame,
The first one to say goodbye
is looked as the one who did not
want to hold on.
Amazingly two are feeling the
same but yet wait for the other
to end it because of having the
pride of not wanting the family
to feel they are to blame.
But yet no one wants to be the
first to say goodbye.
It's like the mirror looking back
to point the finger, and deal with,
the guilt, hurt, and pain of
children, and family making excuses
to blame but it's okay don't
worry about what people say,
if it's what you want to do feel
no shame.

Faith

I am a bird, who has lost a wing but I need to
fly to be free. I have lost a wing to move on
no way to capture food to grow and live on.
I hold on to my faith but this wing has got me
bound my faith is gradually fading don't know how long
I will be around.
In life we all go through the test but we must stay in good
faith.

Seasons

Life can be full of seasons
have you ever classified yourself as a season?
Today I am winter coldness as we cover up to protect
ourselves to keep warm it's like a state of confusion
Here I am beginning to bloom into spring
for the season has changed so now I am blossoming
to begin a new some rainy days some sunny days, yes, this
is true life have you battling good days and bad days. I stand
today as spring can't predict how the days gonna be,
For summer is now here everything bloomed with beautiful
flowers of colors, sun shining all bright too hot to handle for all
the coats and jackets are gone a release until the change begins
again, now I'm fall blowing like the winds, leaves escaping to a state
of nakedness, just bare until the next season comes and another
change begins to appear, Some days up, some days down, some happy,
some sad, but I meditate on it's a new season, it's a new day if you
stay focused on the good it can be a part of your day.

In loving memory of my daddy, Frank Woods,

My dad whom I miss dearly, but I know he sees me and looks down at me even though his earthly days are no longer here but in a resting place of peace, May 26, 2003.

If I could say anything today, it would be I am so grateful for the teachings, values, morals, spiritual upbringing, and discipline that many look at as abuse today, but if it had not been for those disciplinary actions—yes, belt, I'm proud of it—where would I be today?

Supported his family till death took him apart, thirty-seven years of marriage to his family.

Gone but never forgotten.

CPSIA information can be obtained
at www.ICGtesting.com
Printed in the USA
BVHW031023050320
574205BV00001B/125

9 781648 269899